Merry Christmas
1978
with love,
Jack, Kevin & Donna

978
Texas Shelf

LAND AND CATTLE

LAND AND CATTLE

Conversations with Joe Pankey, A New Mexico Rancher

by Jack Parsons and Michael Earney

Foreword by Brant Calkins

Photographs by Jack Parsons

UNIVERSITY OF NEW MEXICO PRESS   Albuquerque

Library of Congress Cataloging in Publication Data

Pankey, Joe, 1892–
  Land and cattle.

  1. Pankey, Joe, 1892– 2. Ranchers—New Mexico—Biography. 3. Cattle—New Mexico—History. I. Parsons, Jack, 1939– joint author. II. Earney, Michael, 1937– joint author. III. Title.
SF194.2.P36A33   636.2′0092′4 [B]   78-56950
ISBN 0-8263-0491-5

© 1978 by the University of New Mexico Press. All rights reserved.
Library of Congress Catalog Card Number 78-56950.
International Standard Book Number 0-8263-0491-5.
First edition

Composed by the University of New Mexico Printing Plant
Printed and Bound by North Central Publishing Company
Designed by Dan Stouffer

This book is dedicated to the New Mexican cattleman.

ACKNOWLEDGMENTS

We would like to thank Brant Calkin and the Frontera del Norte Fund of the Sierra Club Foundation for helping make this project possible; Harvey Mudd and Second Porcupine Press for their generous help, encouragement, and valuable criticism; Eleanor Caponigro for her initial layout of the book, her exacting eye, and her constant support; Michael Tincher, who beautifully printed the photographs and was a friend throughout; and Rosalyn Santiago, who worked long and hard at transcribing and typing. We would also like to thank our partner in Blue Sky Productions, Arthur Dunkelman, who struggled along with us; and most of all we would like to thank the Pankey family for their generosity of spirit and of time.

"Over the greater part of New Mexico it is possible in only one way to collect the land's scanty annuity—by grazing. Ages ago, the Sky Powers determined that the domain should be a possession of ranchmen, and so denied formally most of it to agriculture, manufacturing, and the other pursuits of civilized men."

—Ross Calvin, *Sky Determines*

FOREWORD

The Sierra Club is an organization dedicated to preserving the environment. The work that went into this book was partly sponsored by the Sierra Club Foundation's Frontera Del Norte Fund. Why, you may wonder, would such a group lend its support to a book about Joe and Reuben Pankey, a New Mexico ranching family?

I see this book as a gladiator's salute, a lament, and a celebration.

We began as gladiators, Reuben Pankey and I, at odds over the future of the mountain lion, the need for land-use planning, the administration of the public domain. Through those encounters grew a sense of respect and then of brotherhood. Reuben and the other Pankeys did not so much take arms *against* the environmental concerns I represented as they fought *for* a way of life. The more I learned of that way of life, the more my respect grew for them and their heritage. We will contest again, I'm sure, but this book is a salute between combatants, a recognition that flint striking against steel can produce warmth and light.

The lament is for what is passing. When the West was won, a way of life was lost. The Pankey heritage of land and cattle could only be created once, could last only so long as the conquest was in progress. Having won the battle, the ranchers could only lose the peace. Their life-style could not survive forever. Ironically, the Pankeys have been hospitable to some of the changes that have come in recent years. Two inanimate objects sum up the story: indoors, a forty-year-old saddle, seasoned by the sweat of man and horse and hanging dusty in the tack room; outside, Joe Pankey's Honda tricycle, its noise filtering through the weathered walls. Maybe what is new is better, but there was an integrity to what is being lost. A little of each of us goes with it.

But there is no need to lament the spirit of the Pankeys. It is bright and unquenchable. It is the product of freedom; it is fearless, joyous, and it comes from the heart. It is not diminished by time and it thrives on adversity. The pressures bearing down upon it in today's world may indeed be severe, but it continues to survive and deserves to be celebrated.

Brant Calkin
President, Sierra Club, 1976–77

PREFACE

The Pankeys of New Mexico

Land and Cattle tells the story of a long-time New Mexican rancher, Joe Pankey. It shows what a cowboy's life is like and how it was to grow up in this vast, dry land at the turn of the century. Through Joe's words we get a glimpse of times gone by, the recurrent meeting of the old and new and the changes that inevitably occur.

Joe Pankey, the first of four brothers, was born on August 1, 1892, in Doña Ana County, New Mexico. His father, R. B. "Rube" Pankey, a highly respected rancher who became lieutenant governor of the state, had the distinction, among others, of trading cattle with Pancho Villa. Joe's mother, Anna Cavitt Pankey, came west after the Civil War with her father, a southern landowner who lost his leg at the Battle of Gettysburg. From the first, Joe and his brothers learned the skills of a cowboy—riding, mending fence, doctoring cattle, branding, repairing machinery, and all the other practical accomplishments necessary to run a ranch.

In 1916, Joe married Edith Armer, daughter of a ranching family near Kingston, New Mexico, in the Black Range. Kingston was the site of impressive silver strikes in the 1870s and 1880s, but lost its importance and began to fade away as the price of silver declined.

When Edith came to Joe's modest ranch over fifty years ago as a young bride, there was no electricity or phone or automobile. The nearest town, Hot Springs, was thirty miles away. Often Joe spent long periods of time out on the range caring for his cattle. In this solitary environment the two Pankey children, Reuben and Josephine, were raised.

Today, telephone and electric lines cut across the open range to the ranch and a pickup truck can make the run to Truth or Consequences (formerly Hot Springs) in under an hour. The ranch now stretches out over thousands of acres. A sweeping landscape of grass, saltbrush, and mesquite, it extends to the Rio Grande on the east, runs close by the town of Monticello and Alamosa Creek to the south and west, and borders the San Mateo Mountains to the north. In addition, there are extensive grazing rights in the Cibola National Forest bordering Pankey land. The small five-room adobe house that Joe built, in which he and Edith raised their family, now stands empty behind a new and unpretentious frame house. The stock pens nearby often are full of sleek Herefords or a Charolais-Brahma crossbreed.

Five miles away from the ranch headquarters, Joe's son, Reuben, lives with his wife, Joyce, in Red Rock. Reuben is an equal partner in the ranch and shares the management of it with Joe. Reuben has also served as president of the New Mexico Cattle Growers Association and spends a good deal of time in Washington, D.C., as a committee member of the American National Cattle Growers. Josephine, Joe and Edith's daughter, though living in California, is still part of the ranch operation and is involved with the family corporation, in which all family members are included.

LAND AND CATTLE

Now this Joe Nations was kinfolk of ours and he had a big cattle ranch, and that's how my name became Joe. My father worked for him as a young man. They had lots of cattle over in the Sacramento Mountains on them big plains, thousands of cattle. My mother and father lived on the ranch there and when I was born my father said, "Well, I would like to name him Joe." And then when he did, Joe Nations said, "I'm going to give him a cow and a calf." A red cow, I remember her. She had a Bar 7 on her, and since then I been in the cattle business all my life.

I went to work at twelve years old. The kind of a boy who never went to school much in his life goes to work, the first thing he has to learn is to take care of himself, take care of his bed and take care of his horse and do a daily work. Don't make no difference what it is. He learns to cook, saw meat, make a bed, and then he goes out in the morning, looks over his ranch, whatever he might find that needs attention—cows, water lines, windmills. Then he comes back and takes care of his evening work. It's the same. Gets his supper, goes to bed. He hasn't had no degree for that. And when he's ready to go on a roundup, like the early days, he has to have seven horses, have 'em all shod, that's his business. Have his bedroll to take with him, have his saddle and all of his equipment and go and be responsible for the man he's working for, his cattle and calves.

They'd put you out on a camp like that one over there. We didn't have no house, had a tent and you stayed there and lived there by yourself. But we didn't think nothing of it, wasn't used to no radio or nothing. Of course, I liked to ride. It was about the only thing we could do to enjoy ourselves. That and work. A young boy learns to ride broncs, learns to take care of horses, learns to take care of a remuda [herd of saddle horses] and all that goes on in a cowboy's life. He never went to school a day for that. He learns from back history. The older ones teach the younger ones. In this day and time, take a man who wants to hire a cowboy. This cowboy wants a house, wants Saturday and Sunday off, insurance, it's just like forty hours a week, nothing else. But when I was a boy, you worked. We thought it was a great honor to work some big cow outfits. We did what they wanted done, we didn't ask no questions. That was it. Had some tough old bosses, wagon bosses. They were sincere about what they were doing and they expected you to be the same. No fooling around. You worked for them. Did what they wanted done, not what you wanted done.

Now thirty, thirty-five years ago, right here at this ranch I could go to Monticello and I'd have to fight off them fellows as to how many I'd want to hire. If I wanted five, I could hire ten, they were all there ready to work. But they got away from all that, the young ones. The old ones died, the others all moved to town, to big towns like Santa Rita, mining towns, or went to California. You can't hardly blame them. Got married, got children, got to get wages. But as far as the old cowboy business, I don't know what's going to become of it, nobody wants to work, not our way. The people today, oh gosh, they just die a natural death.

I worked for different outfits growing up as a young man. And after that I rode broncs for a long time and then went to rodeo. Back and forth 'cause that was the cow business. They didn't have the circuits then, you'd just go and attend one of them. Every year, or eight or ten months, they'd have another one. They hadn't got this rodeo racket, none of that. They'd have a big one in Los Angeles in the spring, and then they'd have one maybe in Montana. I'd go by train, they didn't have these automobiles. We'd go and it would be so many days, and then come back. They didn't have us organized like they do now. You'd go in and you'd enter it; if you won, fine and dandy. If you didn't, you'd come home. It was a real championship. I rode one time for thirteen days, every day. They'd keep chittling out until there was only three or four men left. If you got throwed off you might as well pack up your outfit and go home, because there was no more chance, you was already out. In those days there was no kind of money, just championship. Today they have money. There ain't no championship to it, they got it figured out who's going to win it this year and the rest of these old boys follow along. In those days you was either a bronc rider or you wasn't one.

Those were the days they had the big roundups, two or three months out of the year. We all took part. When I went on my first cattle drive I was ten. We drove 'em from different places, you see. About four miles below Lake Valley there's a station called Ocola, and that was the shipping point. Sometimes we'd have a thousand, fifteen hundred cows. And you'd have to drive these cattle up from the Hillsboro country down to there and sometimes you'd have to hold them a week, be so many cattle there. And that dang town only had thirty-six-foot-long cars, and later on they got the forty-foot-long cars to load the cattle in. And then for a long time that railroad had a limit as to how many they could pull. Sometimes you'd be there and you'd have to wait maybe a week before the train would pull 'em. One time [1915] we got to go to Kansas City, boy that was something, to go to Kansas City with the stock. Thirty or forty cars of cattle, three or four men go with 'em free. You'd go up there and you had your fare back. You'd consign these cattle to some commission company and they'd sell 'em off. People weren't as sharp then about this cattle business, and cattle weren't worth as much either.

About fourteen years now we've been selling cattle to the same man, and his name is Buster Wheat. He's got a place in Emporia, Kansas, he's a big trader, handles a hundred thousand cattle a year—just he and his wife and his son, they're the operators. There's no contract, when the fall cattle come we just send word that they're ready and he sends a truck. The funny thing about it, we don't even talk about the price. We fix up the cattle, Reuben and I, Reuben does the weighing, and soon as the cattle's loaded, started on the road, I call Buster and give him his number of cattle, the weight, and when they should be there. And then he'll call back maybe the next day and say, "Well, I'll send you a check for 'em." And it's always right up to par. He don't ever cheat you, he's an honest man. I wouldn't send him, and Reuben wouldn't send him, one pound over, and I wouldn't send him one calf that he couldn't sell. We send him five or six hundred cattle a year, all good cattle. Now this fall, they'll all be one certain size and they'll probably weigh around three ninety, four hundred pounds.

'Course, we've got some old culls and cattle we take over to Socorro to the sale, but they're hardly ever top cattle. Bad-eyed cow or an old cow, an old bull or a cripple, something like that. Years ago we used to sell a cow to maybe a market down there and they'd buy her and kill her. You can't do that no more. These days you got to go to a Deming or Albuquerque packing company and they're killed and stamped, then they can be brought back.

Reuben Pankey and Joe taking a break during roundup.

Reuben, Joe, and Chane Sterling.

Chane, a neighbor's boy, was hired by Joe to help in the roundup.

Reuben shows Chane how to fix his spurs. A cowboy's equipment always needs looking after.

7

Reuben mends a rope and fixes his bridle.

On a ranch there's always something that needs to be fixed or mended.

For Chane, working with Joe and Reuben is like going to school.

The cattle camp.

The San Mateo Mountains. These mountains are part of Cibola National Forest, where the Pankeys have extensive grazing rights.

Pankey land looking west with the Black Range in the distance.

When I came here [in 1921] we just had these two rooms, there wasn't any more than these two here, this had a dirt floor—it was terrible. But anyhow, the country didn't have these mesquites on it, and up there in the hills there's all that walking cane cactus. Every once in a while it dies out for a spell. It wasn't there when I come here. When I come here it was just grass and greasewood brush. Let me tell you how the mesquites got here. Got here through horses. There weren't any fences between here and the river, and the horses run back and forth. And they go down in the springtime where all the mesquites are, eat up on those mesquite beans and just carry them all over the country. And that's how they got started. Now, they're good feed, mesquite beans, good feed. You see them long beans, did you ever taste one of 'em? When they're ripe, they're sweet. Got a lot of protein in them, got a lot of sugar. Cattle are crazy about 'em, horses too, and that's why they eat them. And those seeds are hard and they go right through the cow or the horse and start again.

The weeds have changed. When I first came here there weren't hardly any weeds in the country, and the big high wind, I guess, I don't know how else they got here, brought in a world of seed, wheat seed, brought in filaree and Indian wheat, all from Arizona. There's other different plants come in, too, I don't know where they come from, but some of them's cow feed and some of them's not. Indian wheat has four or five stalks together and each one is loaded with wheat just like our wheat. They tell me that's what the Indians used years ago. They ground it up and used it. It wasn't here when I got here, it come in since then. I talked with other old ranchers and they say these big high winds that blow in from the west for thirty or forty years' time, high up in the air, lifts this stuff up and brings it in. And brings in other plants, too. And now I'll tell you something about it. It's peculiar. It can just rain all it wants to after the first of the year and this filaree and Indian wheat won't come up. But if we have a wet fall and summer, it comes early. Finest cowfeed in the world. Cows just get mudfat on it.

You can tell a plant that a cow will eat. I pick them all the time when I have my teeth, all the time, pull them up by the roots and crack the root. If they have a taste like radishes or turnips, that kind of taste, it's good feed.

And dry farming didn't do the land here no good. Didn't have enough moisture. Farmers plowed up all the native grasses, then walked off and left it, and then the wind got to blowing on it, kind of swept it off, and all kinds of noxious weeds grew back. That's what happened to that. You can't farm in a country unless it rains a lot or got some irrigation, that settles that, sure does.

We have a permit with the Forest Service, paying for every cow running over there, and we're not supposed to feed any more cattle than is on there. We keep a record. We go in there once a year and take off our sales and our losses. That all comes off. Time you get that off, you'll probably be down below what you're supposed to carry, but the increase brings it back again. Lots of people trespass on it, you know, get more cattle than they're supposed to and put them on. They cause the trouble. No, you go along with the Forest Service, they'll treat you right. Now the way we do it, Reuben and I, we invite them [the Forest Service] to ride along with us. I want them to see what we're doing, how we're doing. If we need any correction, we want to know about it. That's all there is to it. It's like with electric lines, you know, they helped with that, they'll help with pipeline, helped us with wells, all those improvements have helped us both. It's our livelihood and their improvement. We keep the same amount of cattle there as on the Forest Service land because you get to doin' that, it's fenced, you know, otherwise first thing you know you're trespassin'. Like we take our bulls and sell them and put on new bulls every year. Sell off a bunch of old bulls and then we replace them with new bulls, but we tell the Forest Service about it so they have the bull number. And your bull number is supposed to be so many cows to a bull. And it takes four bulls to a hundred cows. That's supposed to be, but you can have more and you need more in the mountain country. If we had all these cattle in one flat pasture that would be enough.

Oh, there's nothing wrong with things now, you've just got to cooperate with people. When I was a boy you didn't have to cooperate with nobody, you stood on your own two feet. But now it's different and I like it that way. People cuss the Forest Service but we get along with them real well. They're a great help. Taking care of the ranges so's your grandchildren can live on them same as I can, that's the purpose, absolute purpose. Lots of people so selfish they don't want to give up.

One thing that happened was that it [the public land] was overgrazed. Everybody dumped down as many sheep and cattle as they could get a hold of and that's all there was to it. Didn't know any better, just selfish, just had more cattle, more sheep, more this and more that. It used to be a great thing for a man to say, "Why I got two thousand cows!"

Many, many years ago, that's all there was, just cattle, there weren't no mines, a cowboy wouldn't think about working in a mine, good golly! If he was raised on a ranch in Texas, he'd expect a job on a ranch here. And all the boys that was raised up like we were, that's all they knew was ranches, nothing else. That's the only thing they could depend on. Good wages, thirty dollars, that sort of thing. There was no place to go, didn't have no excitement. Isolated, yes sir, it was. Hillsboro was the county seat and Kingston was an old mining town. Went down when silver went down. And Hillsboro went down. They were all silver mines. And they had a freight line come up to Lake Valley before the silver mines came, a regular freight line. Poor fellows didn't do nothing else but freight teams, haul all the provisions.

Up at the head of Monticello Creek, there's a big spring called Ojo Caliente [Hot Springs]. The army, they had a big fort, Fort Ojo Caliente, in the early days after the Civil War. They had all these troops down there watching the Indians. They had different kinds of forts, Fort Craig, Fort Selden, all along the whole country they had forts full of soldiers. Well, they had this one up there. And all those young fellers got mustered out of the army and this Monticello Creek had Spanish people along there, just living along there. Then, of course, when them fellers came out they married them Spanish girls. There were Irishmen, Germans, and Frenchmen, the Hills, the Bourquets, the Sullivans, the Bergers, the Schaeffers, but they all married those Spanish girls. And they took up this land along the creek and made 'em farms and established the town of Monticello. They settled there, and the second generation did the same thing. Married back and forth and all this and that. They used to have a big winery up there. A Frenchman named Bourquet, he took up a piece of land and planted these vineyards. The rest of them raised corn. And they grew up their families and finally they just evaporated. Monticello had too many people, the depression came along, one thing after another, lots of them had stock and ran 'em all over the country and when the government came along putting in the Forest and BLM land, they couldn't run everything they wanted to free, you know. Well, that cut down on their livelihood. Couldn't establish nothing 'cause they didn't have nothing to establish on. Only thing, we had this little town of Monticello and they all farmed over there. 'Course some of their boys got on this WPA, one thing or another, and then they just sat down, didn't do much, got a little money in, and a lot of 'em died, some went to California, or anywhere to get a job, and stayed. The old land is falling to pieces over there. It's kind of a ghost town, now. I tried to buy it, Reuben and I both. I say "I" 'cause whenever I do anything, it's both of us. But it's their old home and they dream they're going to come back to it someday. Now, I'll give you a little illustration. Up north, in those little old Mexican farms, you see patches up there, little pieces of fence about that wide running up there, and another one, and another one, and another one. Well, the main man, maybe their great-grandfather, homesteaded that place. Maybe it was a hundred, or a hundred and sixty acres, or maybe eighty, that's the original piece of land. He didn't want no three-sider then. He raised a family, then he wanted to give each one of them a piece of ground, then the next one he raised a family and he took his piece of ground and started cutting it down. And that's the way it goes. But they won't sell it. And they always think they're going to come back. Their ancestors are all dead, and the people that own it, they work in California, El Paso, or Las Cruces and they dream about coming back.

In the early days it was John Cross's outfit, a California outfit, that came here and settled all the country from Cuchillo clear to Hillsboro. The river [Rio Grande] turns off to the right through their country. They had sixty thousand cows, can you imagine? They brought horses, drove 'em here from Lower California. And the land, they had lots of land, all up and down these creeks that the people lived on, that was their land. The place where the hospital is down there [Truth or Consequences], that was their land, and all down the river was their land. And what they did, they come in and just file, file claims. I think it was 40-acre tracts at that time, then it was increased to 80, 160, 320, 640. That's the way the land was laid out, that's how they settled the country.

When I was a boy, the museum in Hot Springs [Truth or Consequences] was just a slick hillside. Weren't any houses. There was brush arbors. But the spring then was right where that dripping spring is [Geronimo Springs]. It boiled right out of the ground. Well, people come there in wagons and they built those big brush arbors for shade and they let the horses run. All the town now was just water down there, cienegas [swamps], tules [bulrushes], and grass, and our horses went down there to graze. And they camped right along there. And the first thing they done, they took some old willows and built an old arbor as a bathhouse. Put a little roof on it and a door, and you went in there and bathed and they'd have to wait until you come out, and the next one would have to wait, and the next one would have to wait, and that's the way it went on.

People about that time started to build Elephant Butte Dam and that's what drew the people there. They couldn't go and sell anything up by the dam, liquor, that kind of thing. They had to be seven miles from the dam. That's how the bars come down there. They moved down close to the dam so the people could come off work and drink. A lot of them bootlegged up there all the time. And that's how that old town [Hot Springs, now Truth or Consequences] got started. And they had a merchant move in there by the name of Goetz, who put up a store. And then a doctor moved in there, Dr. Frieze, and then Van Winkle put up a little store, a little grocery store. It was all there on the main street, 'cause down below was boggy. And then people come in for a long time that had squatter's rights. I had one of 'em up on the hill. Then the government come in, surveyed the thing all out, and gave each one of us a patent to that squatter's right. And then they made a map, surveyed the town, got it regulated into streets, alleys, and so on, but the first part was like a cowboy camp. Then, of course, people began to come in, bank came in, and people came in and would build a little home and it just kind of built up. And then they moved the county seat down there. That's what happened. They started the dam about 1908, 1909. See, they had a railroad into the dam to haul the stuff in, then they tore it all up.

The Camino Real, that's the old Spanish trail, went right up the river. Wasn't no road then, I mean when they [the Spanish] come here. See, they come up across the El Paso, came up the Jornada and into Socorro, and they crossed and that's where they all stopped. Socorro means a place of rest, doesn't it? They all give out there. Then they just kept creeping on, some of 'em kept creeping on, till they got to Santa Fe. Every place where some of them give up, they made a little settlement. Then they got to Santa Fe, that's as far as they could go. They stopped there. With every little town they stopped. From those towns they ventured out and got little ranches and little farms, just settled there, wherever.

Mesquite, Mormon tea, and creosote cast shadows on the Pankey range. These hardy growths establish themselves on land depleted by overgrazing. Both cows and horses will eat mesquite beans, but won't touch Mormon tea or creosote.

The Pankey Ranch headquarters is located at the foothills of the San Mateo Mountains in the harsh, dry land of southern New Mexico.

On the right is the original adobe ranch house, with the new frame house behind it. It is here that Joe and Edith Pankey have lived for over fifty years. Reuben and his family, who live five miles away at Red Rock, are their closest neighbors.

Joe rides his horse every day, but he prefers the convenience of his Honda for getting around the ranch.

Two of the Pankey horses waiting to be saddled up.

The Charolais-Brahma cattle have learned to follow the sound of the Jeep's horn in order to be fed "cake" from the back of the vehicle.

The old adobe and the new ranch house, both built by Joe.

Joe riding during a rodeo as a young man.

Souvenirs of the Pankey family in the old adobe home. The Pankey Flying X brand is in the center.

Joe during roundup in 1914. He's seated second from right.

Detail, Joe's office.

Joe's desk.

Reuben's Mexican spurs.

Joe has long been a member of the Sierra County Sheriff's Posse.

Trophies that Joe has won.

Steer heads mounted in the old adobe house.

Photographs of Joe, Reuben, and Mrs. Armer, Edith Pankey's mother, in the office of the old ranch house.

Mrs. Armer was the "Angora Goat Queen of the United States." This photo was found in the Winston town museum.

Joe talking about the old days.

Farm on the way into Monticello.

Main Street, Monticello. This once busy farming community, not far from the Pankey Ranch, is now nearly deserted.

La Alamosa Bar, Monticello.

Monticello Public School.

Deserted adobe with irrigated field in Alamosa Creek above Monticello.

Deserted house, Alamosa Creek.

New settlers—a tepee overlooks Alamosa Creek.

Junked car being used to shore up a bank on the Alamosa Creek.

Hillsboro was once the county seat and one of the many successful silver-mining towns in the area. Now it is being resettled as a retirement town. Hilton, another nearby mining town, where Joe Pankey was born, no longer exists.

Old courthouse, Hillsboro.

Old jail, Hillsboro.

Pump house, Hillsboro.

Marshall Bath House, Truth or Consequences (formerly Hot Springs), New Mexico. Natural hot springs in the area have been used for centuries by Indian, Spanish, and Anglo alike for healing and therapeutic purposes.

Hot Springs Bath House, T or C. In 1950, Hot Springs was renamed Truth or Consequences after Ralph Edwards's popular television show.

When I was a boy, there was a lot of wildlife, but there wasn't any game protection and people killed 'em all off. Then they created the Game Department and they did pretty well for awhile. Now they're not doing much good. They killed off all the game, people have. When I come here, there was very few deer, very few antelope, because people hunted them. And then Judge Nesbitt began the Game Department in Santa Fe. One day I got a letter: "Come up here in Santa Fe, I want to talk to you." Well, I went up there, went up on the train, long time ago. I went to see him and he said, "This game's getting so scarce, where would you think ought to be a good refuge down in your country?" I said, "You're talking to the right man, my range." "All right," he said, "I'll send a man down there, you go with him and mark what you want." And I did that. We put a yellow stripe, a black stripe, and a red stripe. Three long bars like that. Inside of that would be the refuge. There's still one of them on the big rock up there. And we marked it all out. I said, "I'm gonna close this for twenty-five years." And he said, "You see one man in there and you report it." And we just had a few little old deer here. We're down to the same thing now, to the very same point. And I want to tell you that the game that grew up here—great big old bucks, you'd see eight or ten of them in a bunch, and the does—they were gentle, they weren't wild. Nobody'd shoot 'em and we'd just ride right along, they'd be up on a hill there standing. And I'd just got enough accumulated for these big bucks to go out of this refuge onto other ranges where they could be hunted. Well, I thought that was what was going to happen. But old man Nesbitt got out of the deal at that time. Hunters just couldn't stand it any longer, after twenty-five years they threw it open. Now if they had put a limit on some of those hunters it would have been fine. You know, shoot an allotment. And boy I want to tell you that they came from every goddamned state in the Union. They heard about it, you know. They knew about it. And they killed deer here until you couldn't rest. Just big packs of people came. They'd all get big bucks 'cause they were easy to get. Just like shooting down them cows there. Then they threw the doe season open. They slaughtered those does and then they closed it for a year or something like that. Then they opened it again. Now it's open, and the hunters just comb the country. There'll be a gang of men, I've seen 'em here. They just go so far apart and just comb the country. When the old deer come up there, they're going to find them. They go across there, by God they'll kill them over there. He go thataway, they'll kill him. No chance in the world for them. Got these high-powered rifles. Deer can't get away and they're just down to nothing. By God, you used to see 'em every day. But now they're just selling the license but they're getting rid of the deer.

They've stopped trapping the antelope. They're kind of increasing now. But antelopes are funny animals, you know, they don't stay in the same place all the time, they roam around. They get in a band. I saw seven of 'em just yesterday morning. They go around this mountain, this big high mountain, clear back to the St. Augustin Plains, then they'll come back down here and make that big circle. If it's a good spring, well, they'll come down there in the spring if it's good Indian wheat or filaree. By damn, they'll be there harder than a bunch. Another time, there won't even be one. They go someplace else. There's a bunch stays down here sometimes, but not much. But deer don't do that. They stay in one place. They roam around a little bit, but they don't make any big circle like the antelope do. Just go from here to the river, then back to these hills, and that's as far as they'll go.

And the bears, they got them too, you know. Not much chance for anything to increase. And the mountain lions, if they hear about them, they'll be on their trail, too. They haven't got a chance. Quail, they do the same thing, and pigeons. The hunters, sometimes they tell me to get off my land. Oh, I have a helluva time with 'em. That's what people think you know: "We're the people." They don't respect nobody. Now another thing about public lands, we just have the right to grazing, and the rest of it belongs to "we, the people" for multiple use, which is all right, that's what it's for. But somebody walks up and don't respect that right, they don't respect it, what they're supposed to do is hunt. They come in, tear down the country, throw down their tin cans, abuse it, which hunting's all about, that's their privilege. But where deer is concerned, they throw down old beer cans and paper, the same things they throw out of their car. And when I come here, I didn't know what a beer can looked like. That's all happened last ten years. People come up here, they're not hunters, respectful hunters. They come up here, have a good time, a little recreation. Drinking and fighting and whores, one thing or another. Tell you the truth, that's the way it goes. The hunting's the excuse but it's their recreation.

Once we went up the creek here, 'course it was cloudy, got up about five or six miles, saw the snow coming, but John [a ranch hand] and I didn't think nothing about it, just kept on gathering cattle, and boy, it was blowin' and snowin' like a blizzard. We stopped to build a fire and thought, "Maybe it'll quit," but it didn't, and John, he got awful cold, 'cause he wasn't well clad, you know. I told him to put on a pair of leggings but he said, "No, I'm all right." But he got awful cold and I got a little scared 'cause he was kind of shaky, so I said, "Let's turn the cattle loose and go home." Because it was snowing too bad, and when we got back, I said, "John you go home. Get to town while you can still get out of here," and he did. And that evening I went down to fetch the cattle, still a lot of snow and blowin', you know, and I finished up and went back to the house, but I'm used to that. I know how to take advantage of it, not that I'm so smart but I was raised with it. When you go out, take some clothes, don't be afraid to take them along. Coats, tie 'em on your saddle, you may not look like a cowboy but you sure stay warm. One time I pretty near lost a man up there. We had a bunch of cows and calves and we were going to bring them over here, and I was well clad and, by God, comes up one of these storms and it was blowin' and I got pretty cold. We got down off the hill in the canyon and he stopped. And I looked at him and he'd turned pale, and I got down to light a fire. I got some snow and went to rubbing him, his face, his hands, he had pretty much fallen down dead. I kept him quite a ways back from the fire and I kept rubbing snow on him. In a few minutes, I believe he'd a died.

In that day and time they didn't build all this camping equipment, they didn't have it. We made our camp by cutting up some brush and leaning up some poles and putting the brush over it to make a windbreak. We used to roll up some old rocks and gunnysacks, got the campfire going, got the stones real hot and put them near our bed to keep warm.

Another way we used to do it, if it was awful cold and freezing, we'd make a little fire in a great big place like this and put a camp bed down there. Get that ground hot and rake off all the coals and put our beds there. But those things, nature just tells you what to do. Just what you're raised to do. If you like it, don't make no difference. What you don't like, there's no success, ain't that right? Put all your mind on it, all your physical strength, if you like it. If you don't like it, it won't amount to anything. You got to like a thing to make a success of it, that's what I think.

Well, I'll tell you what happened to me one time. We were running a bunch of wild cattle and I was riding a big gray horse, boy he was awful snaky. My brother and I, we were running two big old steers down along a slope, a lot of big old juniper trees all along this slope, and this was in the wintertime. I was riding this horse and the son-of-a-bitch got away from me and got going right down this long slope and there was this big juniper tree that had a big limb sticking right out. Well, we were rushing so goddamn fast I tried to turn this horse, but he wouldn't, he just kept on going. I knew I couldn't dodge this limb 'cause it was too big, and I couldn't get off, so I pulled his head up and he hit this big limb. And it caught his head just right and caved his head in. If it didn't I wouldn't be here today.

I had another horse drag me under a tree, he was a snaky horse, too, he dragged me about the length of this house. Boy, that was something else, he kicked me five times in the back. He had on new shoes. Kicked me right here, right on the butt. He left plenty of shoe there, you know. But when I hit the ground, you see, he was running and kicking, and I turned my head over so he couldn't kick my face. And finally I came loose. And he went on and, oh boy, I was bruised up. And I stayed there a little while. And nobody was around there and I finally walked up on top of the hill. I had a Luger, I couldn't go no further and I shot and they [the other men] could hear it and they started coming. My brother had a horse, so I climbed up behind and went home. But I never did find that horse with the saddle on him. That was in, oh, about May I think, and we looked and looked and looked, every day we looked for that horse, and we couldn't find him. He got tangled up with them riding reins and starved to death, and died with his saddle on. And a hunter done found him the next year, found the saddle on the horse. But that's about as close as I ever come to gettin' killed, right there, gettin' dragged to death.

And one time we were up there in Colorado Wild Canyon, caught a big old maverick bull, a big one. Well, I'm going to tell you about this bull. I had this big old mare, and I had a pack mule, and you know what a cayuse is? It's a square pack box you put on a mule. We had all our truck and everything in it, and the wild oats were about this high. This old bull kind of stopped, and we held up the dogs and cattle to see if we could get him started, and this little mule was just going along just eating them wild oats. Then the mule stopped, stopped eating them wild oats, and that bull saw him and Godalmighty! You couldn't even see him. He hit this damn mule right in the rump and just turned him right flat upside down on top of these boxes and his feet in the air. 'Course that old bull couldn't hurt him 'cause he had his horns shorn off. And we finally got that old bull off him and got the mule up and packed again. But the funny thing, the mule would go way ahead and everytime we stopped, he'd look for that bull.

And we took that old bull out to pasture and kept him there a long time. And the next spring we caught him again. And you know what happened? When we caught him and started out back to the ranch we never had a bit of trouble, he didn't want to fight or nothing, just wanted to go back down to that country. And that happened for three years. And nearly every year he'd go back to where we found him that winter, go back where he was raised, but as soon as we'd get in that area, he'd be ready to come home. That was the first wild animal I ever seen do that. There was always something he wanted to do besides be a wild bull.

Spring roundup in the San Mateo Mountains. Here the Hereford cattle are driven to the corrals at the cattle camp for branding, castrating, and doctoring. Herefords are well adapted to this mountainous terrain and have proved to be a popular beef-producing breed.

Dense underbrush in the sweltering canyons can make rounding up the cattle hard and tiring work. Calves often hide in the shadows, which makes them hard to find.

Cattle are kept moving along the dry riverbed.

Circling from above one of the many limestone formations, Joe chases a stray back to the herd.

Riders and cattle take a short rest.

Reuben fixes fence cowboy-style. This is the kind of task that can't be put off.

Cattle are allowed to move along at their own leisurely pace.

Sometimes, however, they need a little encouragement.

Occasionally, the cowboys will have to wait while the herd regroups.

Many miles are covered over difficult and varying terrain.

There is very little shade. The men must rest in what shade they can find.

Reuben relaxes for a moment.

Then it's time to move on again.

As the cattle are driven near the corrals, they become restive and begin to bunch up.

Joe drives the cattle into the corrals.

Reuben begins to separate the animals that have been branded from those that haven't.

Chane and Alfonso wrestle down a calf to doctor it for worms.

Joe heats up a couple of branding irons.

The Flying X brand.

A sorry old animal that will be sold off from the rest of the herd.

Joe corrals his horse.

Chane and two calves.

Found antlers at the cattle camp.

Water from the well.

Alfonso, the hired hand.

Getting ready for the branding and castrating.

Joe waits for a calf in the chute, a narrow passageway where the animal is held during branding and castrating.

Tools of the trade.

A calf in the chute gets the full treatment: his eyes and ears are sprayed, and he's vaccinated, castrated, and branded.

The time between calves is short.

Steers, the calves that are castrated, get their ears notched at the same time.

A dead calf is dragged off.

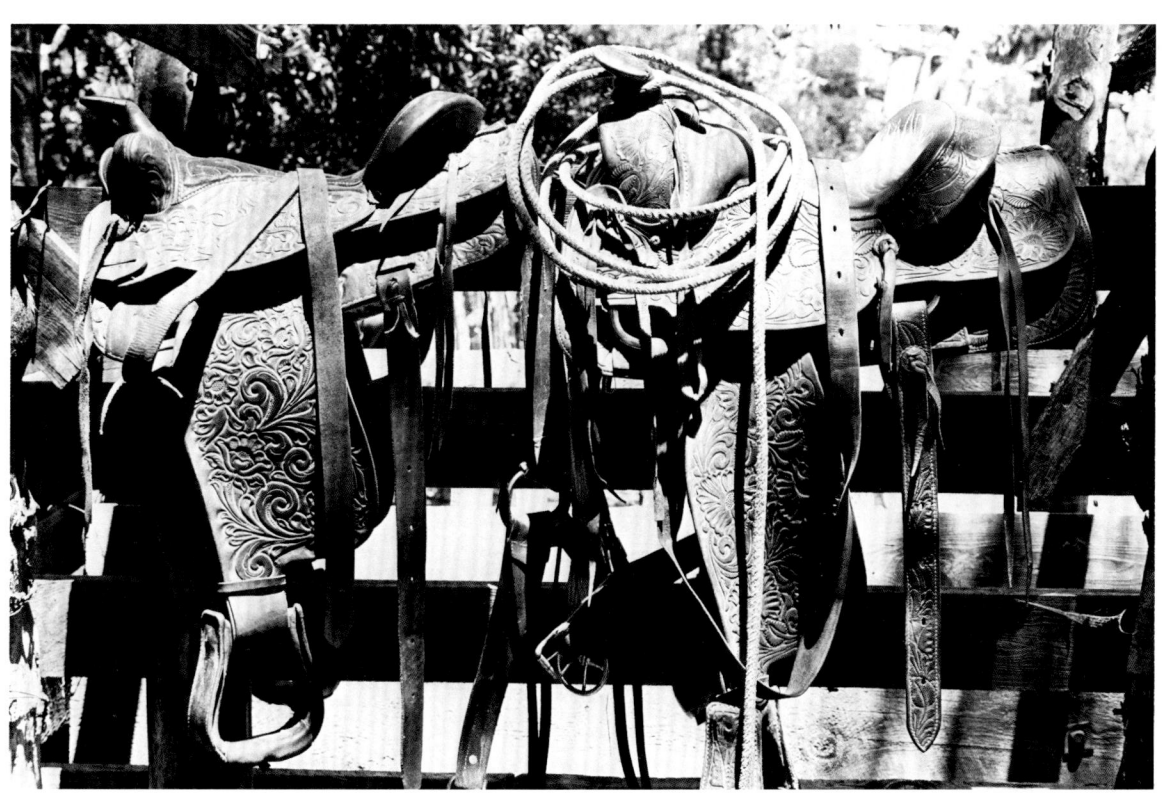

The day begins with Alfonso bringing in the horses that have been left to graze on the surrounding hillsides.

Shoeing horses.

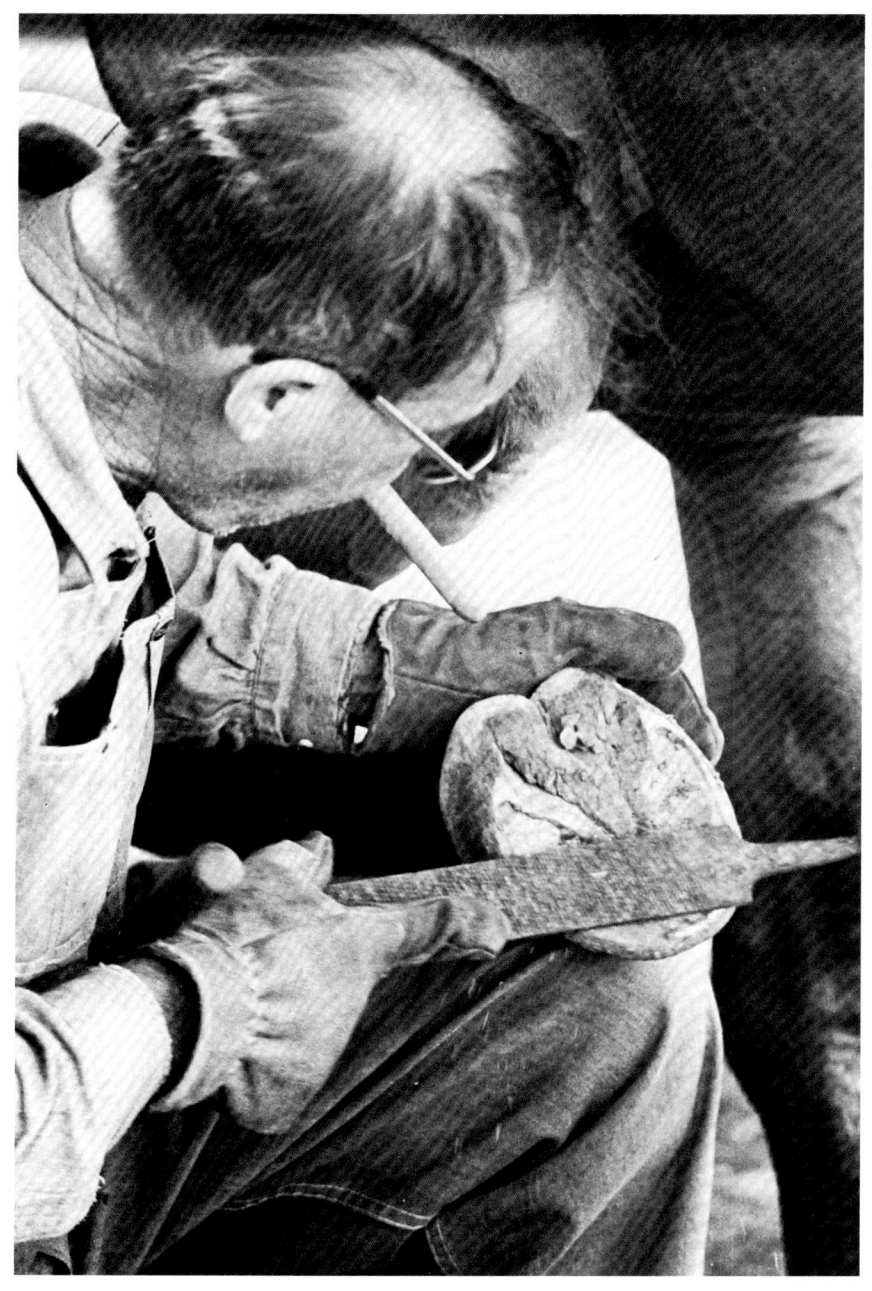

My father, 'course he was a boy when he ran away from home, he was about twelve or thirteen years old. It was during the early days of trail driving, from Texas to Wyoming and back. Yeah, he went up there seven times. That's about all I know about him. Those were wild days. 'Cause he didn't tell us much of his history, you know. My father's people were farmers in Texas, around Austin, and they were good farmers. He just kind of run over school and then just, heck, got to be a cowboy and just on and on until he got to be a cattleman. At that time I don't suppose he made very much money, you know, they didn't pay much. Maybe $30, $35 a month. And after he got through with all of that he married my mother. They were Mississippi people. On my mother's side, they were Cavitts, wealthy plantation people. Had niggers and raised horses, all this and that. And of course when they got through the war they didn't have nothing left. And my grandfather, he was raised a rich boy, but he didn't hardly do anything. He got through the war and was kind of a helpless man, you know, in the way of business, but he managed all right. He got his leg shot off in the Battle of Gettysburg. He came west and went into the cattle business and then my father came, and he and my mother married and started the Pankey family. And I was born in 1892, in the Sacramento Mountains in a little town called Hilton, but there's no more town, it's disappeared. And he was running the Riley outfit down in Las Cruces in the Organ Mountains, and then they sold out, and then when I was about six or seven years old, we moved to Sierra County.

During the First World War we rode twelve miles to get my grandfather the newspaper. It was about the only paper had a little picture in it of the war. And we'd go once a week. He'd look at those trenches, he was a terrible swearer you know, and he'd say, "Look at them goddamn cowards. Little ditches." And I'd say, "How'd you do it, Grandpa?" and he'd say, "Marched up one line, Dixie on one side and Yankee Doodle on the other, like hogs." He was pretty sour on Yankees. One time when we lived outside the little town of Hermosa, there were old retired soldiers there, mostly northern soldiers. Of course, I was raised with them. So my Mama said, "Why don't you take my father up there, I'm going to get some groceries today and visit with the people." Well, every day the old soldiers are sitting under those trees, whittling, talking about the war and all this and that. And I took Granddad up there and introduced him to those soldiers and they were pretty nice to him. I went down to get some things in the buckboard and when I came back, the war had started. He'd found out they were Yankees. The peg leg, he had that off. And boy, he was ready for action! Slam 'em all to death. I got him quieted down and got all my stuff and went back home. And my mother said, "How'd he get along?" And I said, "I'm not taking him no more." She asked me what happened, so I told her I wasn't taking him back, too rank for me. Of course, he was bitter, lost all the power in his leg.

My father was an importer of Mexican cattle. Pancho Villa would deliver them to the border, near Columbus, New Mexico, and about ten o'clock in the morning they'd have the cattle on the Mexican line down on that side and this would be the American side. Hugh and I, that's my brother, he's dead now, we were just young boys, and we were there. Pancho Villa always rode a big sorrel horse. And he never come across the line. He was just standing there. His brother Hipólito done all the counting with my father, eight hundred or a thousand cows or whatever it might be, and then we'd take 'em in from the border about two or three miles. That's as far as we'd go that day, and that night we'd spend right there. After the cattle got across the border Pancho Villa would trust my father with them, and my father would go back that night and pay, pay in cash. Go back to Tilly's place. Well, Tilly has improved this place a lot since then. Where the bar is was just an old Mexican bar, an old adobe room. And that's where my father went and paid him. Pancho Villa, he'd stand up there and he'd buy drinks for everybody, but he wouldn't drink. He had on this pearl-handled six-shooter, big moustache, you know. Of course, Hugh and I, we just sat there and looked at him, our eyes about that big! And Dad and him would go back there, and he'd pay him, and then come back and buy some more drinks. He was a good-looking man but I guess he'd kill you in a minute.

We had outlaws, sure did. My father was shipping horses to Cuba, 1903. Ship them down there and the Cubans were going to break them for their sugarcane fields, you know, plow with them. And that particular time we were gathering these horses, a fellow came riding up. He had a six-shooter. And a mule broke out, a wild mule. This fellow just rode up there, just come out of a clear sky, and he just took care of this mule. Just took that old pistol out and shot around him like that and turned him back. And my father asked him where he was going and he said going through the country. Had on a pair of Okay shoes, a pair of rubber boots, with a buckle, short tops, they were cheap, about the cheapest shoes you could buy. And the next morning my father said, "Well you want to say around awhile?" He said, "Yeah, if you don't mind." My father said he'd give him a job. Well, it was pretty near a month that he stayed until the shipping, and Dad was going to bring ponies and colts they didn't ship back to the ranch up in the *seco*. And he said, "Will you go back up there?" "Yep." And it was getting close to wintertime. He stayed all winter. He stayed there until one day he said, "Reuben, I gotta go." And my Dad knew he was an outlaw of some kind. And he said, "Well, can I help you any?" He said, "No, I just gotta go."

When I was in Hollywood, it was just a little old town. I was doing a lot of bronc riding then and I thought I'd go and I did. I rode broncs in pasteboard corrals. You know, you'd have a Western scene and you'd be ridin' broncs and tear down these corrals and kick through them; well, they're all made out of pasteboard. But that kind of ruined a man. If you ever started that, then kept it up, you had it. If you enjoy something once and want to do it again, that's what happens. Ambition. I was out there when Tom Mix was around. He was the rummest man I ever knew. I'll tell you what used to happen in movies. They used to need a crowd and they'd call out a big crew of people. Well, they just crowded on the street. Many a person went there, girls and boys both, thinking they were going to get in the movies, and all they were was just a bunch of flunkies, you know. Maybe just two or three would be like myself riding broncs. And the rest of them would just stand around and watch you. That's as far as they got in the movies. They'd stay around and go broke. That's where the movie business starts.

Mrs. Pankey, she's a college woman. I take care of the cattle, she takes care of the books, and Reuben takes care of all this government stuff. I don't interfere. We got a pretty good deal here, family, you know. I don't give a dang who you marry, there'll be things come up you have to get ironed out, but then once you do it, it's all right. I don't think there's a couple in the world that don't have that to contend with. I'm honest about it, try to work it out, try to give a little bit. I was twenty-four when we got married. We was raised together. We was raised about thirty miles from one another.

You'll make some mistakes, but eventually you'll get a lot of experience. And that's the best, it surely is. You may not make a lot of mistakes but you'll surely make some. A man never made a mistake never did anything. Always figure that. I make one every day without even trying. You have to be kind of stubborn and know what you want to do 'cause you got so many damn promoters in the deal telling you what to do who don't know a damn thing about it.

People come along and offer folks more money than the place is worth and they take it. They've come to us but we're not ready. We're here, Reuben and my daughter, and we kind of want it to stay in the family unless something happens. I'd like for them to keep it because I made it. But Reuben, he's the last Pankey boy, and that'll be the end of that. That's just the way it goes.

Dudley, an old cowboy friend of Joe's, joins another roundup on Pankey range bordering the Rio Grande.

Joe seeks out strays.

The Charolais-Brahma crossbreed cattle are more adaptable to harsh terrain than the Herefords and can go longer without water.

Cattle gather near one of the few wells on this part of the range. Elephant Butte Lake can be seen in the distance.

One of the Pankeys' prize Brahma bulls.

Joe drives some cows toward the corral. In the background are the San Mateo Mountains.

This Brahma-Charolais mixture is wilder than Hereford cattle and can be dangerous and unpredictable.

The cattle are driven into the corral. The Fra Cristóbal Mountains are in the background, and behind them the White Sands Missile Range.

Dudley with calves. The sorting begins.

The suspicious cattle are gently eased into the corral. In the background, the steep gorge of the Rio Grande runs along the base of the Fra Cristóbal Mountains.

Dudley holds the gate open as calves are separated from their mothers.

John, one of the hands, tries to separate a calf and a cow.

Sometimes a cow will follow her young right into the chute.

Joe counts his cows.

Joe gives out his orders.

Lunchtime.

Joe and Dudley share a story.

Time for a cigarette and then back to work.

AFTERWORD

We first met Joe during the summer of 1975 at the Chamber of Commerce in Truth or Consequences, where he was helping organize the yearly fiesta and getting ready to ride, as he had for years, in the parade. We were filming along the Rio Grande and were looking for a working ranch to include in our film. Joe generously offered to let us use his ranch and to film whatever we wished. The two days we spent with him convinced us that this man had a wealth of experience and stories to be shared. Here was someone directly involved in shaping the character of New Mexico, someone who at the age of eighty-three did not accept the safe haven of retirement but continued to "pay his dues" each day to keep his ranch and business operating smoothly. And perhaps most important for us, here was a real cowboy, a man who had spent his life with ranching and cattle.

It was another year before we were in a position to approach him for a book of oral history. Busy as he was, he again generously offered his time. As we began to participate in the activities of the ranch, our respect for Joe and his family grew. Theirs is a hard, demanding life. Fence must be mended, pumps fixed, cattle chased and rounded up. There are long hours in the saddle in every kind of weather and the absolute need to be able to fix, mend, or build whatever is necessary. Above all, there is a sense of independence and self-reliance, a basic understanding that there is nobody to take care of you if you don't take care of yourself. If the life is hard, it's also filled with its own kind of quiet pleasure and surprise.

I can remember riding out in the early morning into the San Mateo Mountains and suddenly realizing how fresh and alive everything was. There was the feel of the horse under me riding up the steep trail, a hawk circling in lazy spirals to the east, piñon and sage clean and clear in the early light. There was the enjoyment of seeing Joe and Reuben do their work with ease and competence and a minimum of talk and of watching Chane Sterling, the young boy who was helping in the roundup, learn from Joe and Reuben a cowboy's skills. As we rode along, Reuben would remark on the history of the country, the geography, and would point out different grasses and shrubs. And at the end of the day I remember sitting in camp with Joe drinking coffee, tired and sore after a day's riding, just watching the light change as the sun went down.

When we'd go down to the ranch, Joe would make time for us and we'd sit in one of the old adobe rooms while Joe would fire up the stove if it got cold and patiently answer our questions. In editing the tapes and transcripts, we have tried to retain the spirit of what occurred as faithfully as possible. Inevitably, the project had some disappointments. Mrs. Pankey, a warm and generous woman, but also very shy and modest, preferred not to be photographed despite the urging of her husband and ourselves, a decision we could certainly understand and respect. Putting this book together was for us a delight, and we came away from it with good memories, good times, and the hope that the words and pictures will give others some of the pleasure the making of this book gave us.

Jack Parsons